Mother and Son

Cover Image: Central Park / Angelo Rizzuto, 1906-1967. Library of
Congress Prints and Photographs Division Washington, D.C. 20540 USA
http://hdl.loc.gov/loc.pnp/pp.print
Book Design: Rowan Kehn

ISBN: 979-8-9868994-7-3

Turning Plow Press

For my mother, Mary Currie Austin

Author's Note

While the episodes of this semi-autobiographical story of a mother and son are mainly true to fact, they represent my imagined understanding of moments in time told primarily from the mother's point of view.

Contents

1932

The Ferry

She comes from Nova Scotian men
who pick by pick dig out
company coal till one by one
they wear out limbs and lungs.

She's old enough now to be
one of the women who feed
and clean their children,
comfort the men and themselves.

Like them, she lives in daily fear
of the siren's wail that predicts
more names will be added
to the long tally of untimely deaths.

She prays the Virgin give her strength
to endure the life assigned her.
Doesn't believe her own words.

She watches the women
send the men off to the mines
from her Glace Bay window,
and yearns to answer the demand
of her young, restless body
to belong to another life...

A feeling of absence begins, blurs her senses,
stirs her mind to brew a brand-new thought...

this is me here, that is them there...

She keeps herself secret, seals herself off
from her need to be consoled, afraid
to surrender any hope for change.

On the day she's ready,
she boards a ferry from Halifax
to Boston, one suitcase in hand
toward a future shrouded in fog.

1942

The Limp

'Does it hurt?' the mother asks.

'No. Well, a little bit, I guess.'

No broken bones. No bruises. No way
to know what caused the limp.

She sends the boy to lie down,
rest till supper. Hopes for the best.
Maybe just a one-time thing.
A kink that irons itself out.

At supper she sees the boy's pain,
the timid way he limps, sits at table,
head down, not looking at his parents.

Worries to see the boy shrink into himself
like it's his fault. Recalls how she felt
the day she packed to leave Glace Bay.

Harry, thank God, comes to the rescue:
gives the boy his best grin, ruffles his hair,
does a silly imitation of Bing Crosby.

Oh Christ, she thinks. If the kid can't even
crack a smile at his father's shenanigans,
this is real trouble.

The Operation

'The blood flow to the boy's left hip has dried up,'

the doctor says, 'the ball joint is crumbling fast.'
He tells her they'll have to operate today.

I'm not here, she thinks, the word ringing in her head.
'Today!' she says, 'Why today? What's the rush?'

'The deterioration has already progressed to the degree
that, as of now, any weight put on your son's hip,
there's a good chance he'll be permanently crippled.'

A flash of the boy wasting away in a wheelchair
shudders through her.

'Once the operation's over,' he says, 'the blood
flows back to the ball joint, but then the bone
needs a long time to become solid and strong.'

A long time? What does he mean a long time?
Today, tomorrow, forever? What does he mean?

She throws a what's-going-on look to Harry,
who puts an 'I'm here' hand on her back,
and asks the doctor how long it takes to heal.

It varies case by case, he tells them,
some a few months, others two, three years,
rare occasions could be more.

Three years! If ever she needed to get a grip,
pull herself together, freeze the stab of fear
burning in her stomach, she better do it now.

'You should also know,' the doctor says,
'the boy will be bedridden for however long
it takes for the bone to heal.'

How in hell can he expect a six-year-old

to be off his feet for even one day?
She doesn't like this man. Thinks too much of himself.

'So, when do we get to see him?' she asks.
Aches to do something. Anything she can.

'We'll give you a little time after he's prepped
and before he goes in for surgery.'

Give it a little time, she thinks. Like it's a favor!
Don't I get a say in this? I'm his mother, for Christ's sake.

'He'll be a long time coming out of the ether,'
the doctor says. 'First thing tomorrow we'll send him
to the Peabody in Newton for his long-term care.'

'Newton!' she says. Christ, that's a bus to the trolley
at Kenmore Square, another bus to Newton, then
the whole thing over again. We have to work,
we can't afford the time, never mind the money.

The doctor's sorry but the Peabody's the nearest charity
for families who can't afford full-time home care.

Don't they always do that, she thinks.
Look down their noses at you. Shame you
into thinking it's your fault for being poor.

He advises them it's best to go home and rest;
excuses himself, leaves to operate on the boy.

The glare of afternoon sun shines through
the hospital window.

She's exhausted from lack of sleep when she gets
on the bus for the long trip to Newton. Jittery as hell
from having to wait that night, the whole next day
for the boy to get out of recovery.

She still can't help thinking about the look on the boy's face
when they took him to the operating room.
It's not fear. It's something else. She doesn't know.
Hopes it's just her imagination. She wills herself to go blank.
Clear her mind, keep from falling asleep. Be in charge.
Be there for the boy.

She has to shake herself awake maybe six, seven times
the whole way. God forbid, I miss the stop is the only
thought she allows.

The resolve she feels when she gets off the bus
dissipates when she sees the sign over the entrance.

PEABODY HOME FOR CRIPPLED CHILDREN

How am I supposed to do this without Harry?
Just our luck he signed up for painting ships
not two days before we knew about the boy's hip.

'I hate to leave you to handle the kid alone,'
he'd said at breakfast, 'but at least the money will help.'

She knows it's not only the money.
Knows he's got people over there.

Okay, she tells herself. Forget the war. Keep your eye
on the kid. It's him needs Harry as much as you.

She struggles to make it feel right someone else

9

is looking after her son as she walks up a long slope
of concrete walkway that divides a wide expanse
of perfect green lawn, which helps her avoid the sign
over the entrance.

'How did you like our office manager?' the nurse asks,
as they leave his office for the first visit in the solarium.

'It wasn't fun,' she says.

The nurse gives her what she takes as a knowing look,
and says, 'Never is with that one,' then reminds
the mother the first visit needs to be short,
so the boy can have the rest of the day to settle in,
get to know the other boys in the ward. Tells her
it won't be long before she comes back with the boy.

What is it with me, she thinks, my mind should be
on the kid but I can't get it off that little man
in the office, with his button eyes and bow tie
and his fancy studies, giving me that malarkey,
telling me how worrying for my kid is bad for him.
And then the nerve to tell me I can only see him
one Sunday a month. I mean, Jesus Christ!
One Sunday a month! He's lucky I didn't rip up
those goddamn papers I signed.

She sees another slope of perfect green lawn leading
to woods at the back of the hospital. Thinks how green
Boston Gardens was when all three of them
went for a picnic lunch the Sunday before the boy
came home with his limp.

Oh, Mother of God, she thinks, what's happened?
Why have they got him lying down, flat on his back?

'Let me get you a chair,' the nurse says, lays her clipboard

with the yellow rose on the boy's bed, goes to the far end of
the solarium to retrieve one.

She'd imagined the kid in a wheel chair, but this is worse.
They've got him in a canvas restrainer, sort of like
a corset, strapped down to the metal rails of the bed.

'So...you doing okay?' she asks the boy.

'I guess.'

'You have any pain?'

'No, Ma.'

'They tell you why they put that restrainer on you?'

'They said it was to keep me safe.'

The nurse returns, places the chair by the bed.

'Does he have be like this all the time?' the mother asks.

'Oh no. Only when we move him, and when he sleeps.'

The nurse takes the yellow rose from the clipboard,
hands it to the boy. 'Do me a favor,' she says as she
cranks up the boy's bed, 'keep an eye on my rose
like a good boy while I talk to your mother.'
Nods her head to indicate they should step away.

'He'll sit up like this most of the time,' the nurse says.
'It's important the boy not walk at all till the hip's
completely healed.'

God, can it get any worse for the kid? she thinks.

'Of course, like any young boy, he'll get restless,
thrash around, try to walk, possibly damage the hip.
That's why we keep him restrained at all times.'

I was wrong, the mother thinks. It does get worse.

'In a way, the boy's lucky,' the nurse says.
'We've got some kids here with damaged spines,
a few in iron lungs that can't move at all.'

She places a chair so the mother can sit beside her son,
smooths her uniform, picks up her clipboard,
thanks the boy for his help holding the paper rose,
and says, 'I'll let you two alone a few minutes.'

Sitting bedside unsettles her. No last-minute reprieve.
Their lives in the hands of other people. If ever she needed
the help of the Holy Mother, this would be the time.

'Looks like you'll be here a while,' she says.
Figures it's best the kid knows his situation.

'Yuh. They told me.'

'Did they tell you visits are only once a month?'

'Yuh, I know.'

'Well, too bad that's the way they do it here, eh?'

'Yeah, I guess.'

The boy stares into the woods across the way.

'Your father would have been here if he could
but he had to take work at the navy yard.'

'Oh. Okay.'

'Said it was his way to give Hitler a kick in the bum.'
She doesn't get the smile she'd hoped for.

What do I talk about now? she thinks. She picks her purse up
from the floor to her lap. Never much for small talk, was I?
Take after my da. Couldn't get a word from the man without
he had a drink or two. Coal dust in his lungs didn't help
much either. She sets the purse back on the floor.

'Looks like we're stuck with this mess, huh?'

She barely hears him say, 'I guess...'

Something's wrong here, she thinks. Kid's too calm.
Doesn't bat an eye, takes the news... like what?
Like it's somebody else strapped to the bed.

'Aunt Sally and Uncle Jonesy said to tell you
not to worry, you'll be okay.'

'Oh. Good.'

'Well, Sally cried, Jonesy said to tough it out.'

"Oh. Yuh...."

'Wonder what the food's going to be like here?'

'Me, too.'

They fumble through a little more small talk
until the nurse comes in. Time's up.

She thought she'd be ready for this. Had no clue
she'd feel so paralyzed. Imagines the boy will

disappear if she gets up from her chair.

She takes his hand with such urgency he winces.
She tries to loosen her grip. He won't let go.
She pats their locked hands. The boy's hand relaxes.
She frees hers.

The nurse lowers the bed. Wheels her son away.
Tied down. Flat on his back.

Alone, the empty room seems enormous.

Her eyes throb from the bright stream of sun
through the solarium's tall windows.

She turns away to see her shadow on the floor.
Afraid to move. Afraid to give it life.

Waiting

They're lonely together. Sentenced (as they feel it)
to wait out this first long month.

The days pile up. They grow increasingly apart.
Slip further and further away from each other.

Suppers are silent and gloomy.

Without the kid around for his audience,
Harry's lost his happy-go-lucky self.

She takes on more cleaning jobs. Tries to fight off
a deepening despair. Fills the rest of the days
cleaning her own home. Over and over.

Nothing is real. The apartment's a foreign land.
The boy's room an empty space. The kitchen's
unwelcome. Their bed rented for the night.

She's falling away from herself, becoming
a girl at a window in Nova Scotia, thinking
this is me here, that is them there.

Second Visit

During the long trip to Newton she'd hoped
Harry'd be his old self. Happy to see his son
now the three-week wait is over.
But there's no change. His eyes are dull.

'You go ahead, sweetheart,' he says.
'We don't want to keep the kid waiting.
I just need a little minute, catch my breath.'

Been a while since he's called me sweetheart.
Pray God it's a sign he's coming round.

She leaves him sitting on the bus stop bench.
Walks up the concrete walkway to Peabody.

The boy's so concentrated on what he sees
out the window he doesn't turn to look at her,
doesn't even seem to notice the other families
scattered around the solarium.

'Hey,' she says, softly as she can.

'Oh. Hi, Ma.' The boy looks surprised.

Is it her imagination he'd rather be

looking out the window?

'What's out there you didn't notice I was here?'

'Oh, sorry, Ma. It's just I like to watch the birds.'

'So, you like the birds now, do you?'

'Yeah, 'specially the red cardinals.'

'So, then you know their names, eh?'

'The nurse told me. And sparrows, too.'

'So.' She smiles to cover a twinge of jealousy.
'Getting along with the nurse, are you?'

'She's nice,' the boy says. 'She talks to me.'

'Your father's coming any minute now.'

'Oh, good....' The boy looks round for him just as
Harry bounds through the door wearing a grin.
Makes his way over to them dancing a soft shoe,
singing 'Hawaiian War Chant' like Spike Jones.

Song over, he taps the boy's noggin. Says,
'Knock, knock.'

'Who's there?' the boy asks.

'Sarah.'

'Sarah who?'

'Sarah doctor in the house?'

The boy laughs. 'More, Daddy,' he says.

Harry makes his Eddie Cantor google-eyes,
rolls them around in mock search of doctors.

'Can't find any here. I'll bet they've all gone fishing.
But never fear because your daddy's here
to fix you up with a good old-fashioned belly tickle.'

But when he reaches to tickle the boy he freezes.
Flushes red with fear to see his son restrained,
his hands strapped to the bed.

It takes him a moment to find enough breath
to give the boy a kiss on the head, ruffle his hair.

The boy's confused. She's worried.

Harry had that same red face at the bus stop.

Gone in Sleep

She wakes to find Harry's body beside her in the bed.

She lies still. Refuses to weep him gone.

Her eyes map the contours of his face to engrave him
in the present, wait for him to breathe back to life
and restore the only certainty she's known since
Father Gray deemed her soul free of sin
after first communion at St. Anne's.

Seemingly without having moved,
she sits on the edge of the bed,
staring at the brown and tan plaited rug.

A soft tap-tap-tap on the door. She must have
straightened the covers over Harry's body,
somehow managed to call O'Brien's Funeral Home.

What are you looking at? she thinks,
I don't even know you, do I?
Why is this guy she doesn't know from Adam,
the guy who's here with Tommy Rogan,
looking at her like she's supposed to say something?

Don't you look at him, her mind screams.
as the man helps to get Harry ready.
Don't you look at my husband's face!

She must have called Sally and Jonesy after
she'd called Tommy. They're here in time
to see O'Brien's people take Harry away.

Sally wears a half-smile of condolence
to comfort her baby sister. Jonesy calls her 'kiddo.'

She turns down their offer to go home with them
to Bowdoin Street. She'll grieve Harry on her own.

One side of her bed's empty.

Sirens wail a cave-in. Her pulse beats
to the march of dead back in Nova Scotia.

She grieves until she feels the blood
drained from her body, as if she's the one
in the coffin at O'Brien's.

Later, she wonders how she wound up in a bar
staring at nothing, hearing distant sirens,
holding a Four Roses and ginger.

Then someone asks her to dance.

Funeral Mass

What brings on the tears after Father Ryan says
he's sorry he can't say Harry's name during
Holy Eucharist since Harry's not a Catholic,
is the memory of Harry's grin when he proposed
as they sat on a bench in Boston Gardens
watching the ducks in the pond.

How she feared his answer when she said
she couldn't marry him unless he agreed
to bring their children up Catholic.
How she cried in relief when he said
it would be dandy with him as long as
he didn't have to step inside anybody's church.

There she was then, crying happy, the ducks
gliding through the water. Now the church bells toll.
She cries another way.

Third Visit

She's afraid of the feelings whirling inside her.
Afraid she'll blurt things she's ashamed of.
Too ashamed to pray the Virgin's forgiveness.

I've got to tell him now, she thinks. Get it over.
I wait to the end, I leave the kid in a mess.

Neither one makes any sign of how they feel

when she tells him his father's dead.

'Was it an accident?' he asks.

'No, a heart attack. In his sleep.'

'Oh.'

'So he didn't suffer,' she says.

The boy says, 'Good.' Looks out the window
as if he saw something move in the woods.

'Sister Catherine lit another candle for you,'
she says to no response. 'She'll burn
St. Joseph's down she's not careful.'

Still nothing from the boy.

Oh God, Harry, she thinks, if it was you
made that little joke, the kid would've laughed.

'I brought you a Big Little Book.
It's Tom Mix, the cowboy you like.'

The boy straight off begins to read.

'Father Powers prayed the Holy Mother for you.'

The boy turns a page.

She folds up the bag that carried the book.
Puts it in her purse. 'That's a big deal, you know,
it's not just anyone he does that for.'

The boy lifts his head from the book,
looks to some faraway nowhere.

She can't tell if the sudden flash of anger
belongs to her or to the kid or both of them.

'Sally and Jonesy said to tell you hello.'

The boy stares straight ahead, the book in his lap.
Panic stirs up. She could lose her son for good.

1946

Home

The Window

To ease the August heat she draws the green shade
down to match precise the ten inches of open space
from window frame to spotless sill.

Sitting on a straight back chair she borrowed
from the kitchen to keep the parlor chair clean,
she lights her afternoon smoke from a half full
pack of Chesterfields next to a large amber ashtray
that guarantees not a single ash will fall on the rug.

The boy's been home three weeks now
in their new place on Boston's Berkeley Street,
a second-floor apartment she refers to as home.

St. Vincent's secondhand and the Earle Hotel,
stopping place for whores, are not exactly
the best neighborhood to bring the kid up,
but it's what she can afford.

The smoke, held deep in her lungs, escapes
in a half-sighed release, wafts into the summer air,
fades away like a ghost from her past.
The way she'd like to fade from a world
she never wanted, never imagined
that day she boarded the ferry.

A world where Beacon Hill ladies look down
their noses as you scrub their floors, welfare workers
treat you like dirt, thugs roam the streets.

She knows this resentment is wrong.

Longs to confess. Kneel beneath the Holy Mother.
Pray her forgiveness. Relieve her shame. Receive
the grace of sacrament.

But she can't. She hasn't since... No.
She won't think about that.

Mrs. Silverman, kids in tow, pocketbook held close,
goes in St. Vincent's secondhand.

The radio croons Buddy Clark, singing
'I'll get by, as long as I have you.'

She yearns for a slow dance with Harry,
her face soft with nostalgia.

Then something spooks her. Like someone's
reading her mind, opening her mail.

She wonders how long he's been here.
Shouldn't be here in the first place,
watching her have a smoke at the window.

Kid needs to know some things belong to you.
No one else. Mine is mine, yours is yours.
Keep your secrets, you'll get by in this world.

She doesn't turn her head to the boy,
asks him if he needs something.

'No, Ma. It's just I like the song.'

'Go wash up for supper,' she says.

Some fool on the radio sells something.
She turns it off.

She has no illusions it won't be a hard job.

The kid goes in the hospital at six comes out ten.
No father. A mother he's seen once a month.

The healing process they called it. Well, his bones
healed all right. But we never had a chance
to put ourselves right with each other.
How could we? Six to ten are big years.
Him not able to grow up the way most kids do,
me no way of knowing how to help him.

The Peabody had the most of him.
I had him one lousy half-day a month.

All that, you wouldn't expect the poor kid
to come through the door of a strange house
dancing a hula now, would you?

God, I wish Harry was here to bring
a little sunshine into the kid's life.
Balance out for his gloomy mother.

Two weeks and he's off to sixth grade.
No clue how to handle himself.

She reaches for the pack of Chesterfields on the sill
to help her concentrate.

First thing, she'll walk the boy to school
with a peanut butter, banana sandwich.
Pray Christ he doesn't get in trouble.

Then she'll cross the tracks to Louisville Square.
Mop, dust, clean toilets, polish silver
for a rich Protestant housewife.

After that, she'll take the boy home, feed him
his afternoon snack. Get her mops, dust cloths.
Curse the city dirt. Clean her own home.

First Day of School

The boy is standing away from the others
when she comes to walk him home.
Don't worry yourself, she thinks.
It takes a while to make new friends.

'You didn't eat your sandwich,' she says,
seeing the boy's unopened lunch.
The boy mumbles he's not hungry.

Something is wrong, she thinks.
Tells him children are starving in India.
He'll eat it when they get home.

He's ten. She thinks it better she doesn't
take his hand for the walk home.

'So, how was your first day?' she asks.

The boy says, 'Okay.' But he doesn't mean it.

'First day is always hard,' she says.
'Bet you were glad for recess, eh?'

The boy's response is an empty 'yuh.'

They walk on. The boy keeps his head down.

Her mind races every which way. What's going on?

He's got a secret, doesn't he? Doesn't want me
to know, does he? Well, I'm not going to deal with it
out here on the street for everybody to see.

Home, she puts the sandwich on a small plate,
a glass of milk beside it. 'Here you go.'

The boy takes one grudging bite.

'That's it, that's all you want?' she asks.
Letting the boy know she's annoyed.

'I'm not hungry, Ma,' he says. Pushes the plate away.

Now she's full-blown mad. 'What's wrong with you?
You're ten years old; first day in sixth grade,
you act like a six-year-old in first grade.'

'Jeez, Ma,' the boy says, 'don't blame me.
It's not my fault I'm not hungry.'

Oh Christ. The kid looks like he's going to cry.

What the hell's the matter with me? How could I
go after the kid about a goddamn sandwich?
I knew the minute I saw him it was more
than just the usual first day stuff.

'It's okay,' she says. 'There's no blame here.
You had a bad day, I had a bad day because you
had a bad day. So, what do you say we call a truce.'

The boy nods okay. 'Good,' she says.
'So, you want to tell me what happened at school?'

'I messed up in Miss Cronin's penmanship class.'

'What do you mean you messed up?'

'I wrote out my name and address and how old I was
for attendance like she told us... and then... '

A twitch of pain shows on the boy's face.

How bad is this going to be? she thinks,
then asks him, 'And then?'

'She got mad at me for how I wrote.'

'Got mad at you? Why'd she do that?'

'She says I was supposed to write, not print,
so she could check my penmanship. It wasn't
my fault, Ma, they didn't teach that at the hospital.'

'It's all right. I'll give you a note. She'll understand.'

'The thing is...' The boy looks down at the table.
'The thing is...'

'It's okay,' she says. 'Keep talking, you'll be all right.'

'Oh, jeez, Ma...' he says, trying to hold back his tears.
Then they rush out. Tears and anger together.

'I cried, Ma, I cried. Everybody saw me. All the kids
saw me cry. Some of them were laughing at me.'

He looks at her with such pain, she feels it, too.
She wants to go blank. Wash it all away.
But she forces herself to focus on the boy.

'Tell you what. Never mind the bloody sandwich, eh?

Go to your room. Have some privacy. Give yourself
some time till supper's ready.'

The boy takes a step, starts to turn back toward her,
changes his mind, goes to his room.

She hears his door close. What was that? she wonders.

She'll surprise him and fry up some onions
to go with the salmon cakes.

Jesus, what a day, she thinks. Blows her smoke
into the September twilight on Berkeley Street.

Giving the boy some time for himself was a
good idea. Came out of his room right at five.
Thanked her for the onions. Went right at his food.
Cleaned up after himself without a whimper.
Went back to his room to do his homework.

She turns the radio on to keep herself company.

A sudden sharp pain takes her breath away.
Just her luck, she thinks. Moonlight Serenade,
Harry's favorite from before the war.
She shuts the radio off.

A deep draw on her Chesterfield scratches.

Memories strain to be remembered...
the smile on the boy's face when Harry
sang to him in the bright day of the solarium,
the siren's echo in the dim bar where someone
asked her to dance the very night he died,
the boy again, his pain this afternoon...

A rush of shame threatens to crack her open.

The thought of how the kid stared off
to nowhere when she told him his father died
nags at her, makes her uneasy.

Oh, dear Jesus, is there no mercy?

Some motion out the window catches her eye.
One kid chases another into the alley behind the Earle.
It's a long goddamn way from Halifax, she thinks.
Curses a life that got her into this fix.

Bad Language

Three days and the kid comes home from school
with a dirty mouth.

She's no stranger to bad language. But never
in a million years would she use that word.

She can't bring herself to even think that word,
never mind imagine the way some men do
the things they do. When she was a girl, 'sin'
was the only word she ever heard about it.

She takes a deep breath, gives the boy her best
no-nonsense tone. Tells him she wants an apology.

'What did I do wrong, Ma?' he asks.

'Why'd you call me that bad word?'

'What word?'

'Don't get clever with me; the one you said

when you came waltzing through the door.'

'Jeez, Ma...I didn't know it was a bad word.
That's what all the guys call each other.'

Oh, that's it. She gets it now. It's not the kid.
He really doesn't know what he said.
Somebody's messing with him.

'Who was it taught you that word, eh?'

'That's what Dominic called me, and told me
he'd be my friend, watch out for me, make sure
no one would bully me.'

Just as I thought, she thinks. This Dominic kid
is setting him up. Sweet Mother of Christ, here we go.
First it's swearing, then the smoking and stealing,
then God save us, the gang fights.

The McSweeneys and the Foleys already lost
their sons to that God-awful mess out there,
and she'll be damned to hell if she lets that happen.

'Listen up,' she says. 'If I hear that word in my house
even one more time you'll end up grounded for so long
you won't know one day from the next.'

'Jeez, Ma...'

'And the same goes if I hear from Peggy Foley
or anyone in the neighborhood you used that word.'

'Okay, okay...'

'And stay away from that Dominic. He's nothing but
trouble.'

"Jeez, Ma...'

'Never mind Jeez, Ma. Go to your room till supper.'

She can't tell if he's hurt or angry.
Probably both, just like her.

1949

The Slap

The minute she opens the door, sees the blue uniform,
she gives the boy a quick, hard slap, yanks him
into the house, tells the cop she'll take care of it.
Waits a moment to be sure he leaves.

The boy sits on the parlor couch, his face beet red.

'Ma, I didn't...I—'

'Shut up. Where were you?'

'Up the railroad tracks,' he says, 'watching trains.'

'Why would that cop haul you home
if all you were doing was watching trains?'

'I don't know, Ma.'

'Tell me what you were up to, or you'll tell them
at the precinct, if I have to take you there myself.'

'We were just having fun is all.'

'Cops don't arrest you for having fun.'

'It was nothing, we were throwing rocks is all.'

'You threw rocks at the goddamn train!?'

The boy presses himself into the back of the sofa
like he's trying to get away from what's coming.

'Where the hell are your brains?' she says.

'You could have broken a window. Killed somebody.
They would have sent you away to Walpole.
Look at me when I'm talking to you!'

The boy winces, lifts his head a little.
Not so much that he looks at his mother.

'You're thirteen years old,' she says.
'Don't be a crybaby for Christ's sake.
Sit up straight and look at me.'

The boy lifts his head enough to look at her.

'I'm warning you right now, don't B.S. me.
Who was it throwing rocks with you at the train?'

'I only threw one, Ma, only one.'

'I didn't ask you that, I asked you who was there.'

He tells her it was Tommy Foley and some kids
he brought with him from the projects in Southie.

Tommy Foley, she thinks. No wonder the cop was there.

'So how come the cop nabbed you and let the others go?'

'They saw the cop coming and they ran before I saw him.
I didn't know what to do. I was scared, Ma.'

'Let that be a lesson for you. Don't fall for a glad hand
from the likes of Tommy Foley. People like that
leave you in the lurch every time.'

She tells him he's grounded. Straight home after school.
Full curfew every night this week, and next week, too.

'Make sure you go to confession,' she calls out
as the boy droops off to his room.

Later she peeks in on him.

He's lying on his bed like a ghost of himself
strapped to the rails of his hospital bed,
staring at the ceiling the way she'd seen him
that first day at the Peabody five years ago.

He's still, like a photograph.
Makes no sign he knows she's there.

A cold drizzle blurs the streetlights.
Not what she needs this ugly October night,
an hour after a cop knocks on her door.

She's antsy. In no mood to search her old songs.
The radio hardly plays them anymore, anyway.
What else is there to do but grab a little smoke
for herself. The cigarette scratches her throat.
She pays no mind.

First it was that Dominic kid, now here comes
Tommy Foley, six months out of juvie.

Hanging around tough guys to protect himself
can only lead to trouble. She's never seen a cop who
wouldn't rather haul in a teenager than a real crook.

Is it starting now, she wonders, the time when what's
at home matters less than what's out there?

He took his confirmation vows last week. Says he
didn't like the Cardinal. Can't blame him, who does?
It'll be working papers next. A part-time job. Then poof!
High school's done. Out the door for good.

To what? she wonders. The last thing she needs
is him being marched down to the precinct,
handcuffed like a hoodlum. And you can bet
the whole neighborhood will be watching.

The picture of the boy lying on his bed,
staring at the ceiling, going off
to somewhere inside himself, stays with her.

The problem is how to get the kid
to stand up for himself.

She hears the boy open the fridge door.

Let him have a snack, she thinks. Appetite's
a good sign. 'Don't eat that baloney,' she calls out
'it's tomorrow's lunch.'

1950

Mr. Harrington

Supper's more silent than usual. Not even a smile
when she says he'll look like Clark Gable
if he lets the fur grow on his lip.

Couldn't be he's got himself in trouble.
He's been good since the train business last year.
Been getting A's and B's, still keeps curfew.
Chips in half what he earns as bag boy at Ray's.

No, this is a mood she can't read.

'Is there something bothering you?' she asks,
careful not to let him think she's worried.

He doesn't answer but, from the way he looks,
she guesses he will if she gives him a nudge.

'You don't have to talk if you don't want to.'

The boy says Mr. Harrington, the English teacher,
threw his chair out the window and quit.

'Holy Christ on the cross, why'd he do a thing like that?'

'It was scary,' the boy says, 'he kind of went crazy.'

He tells her a kid named Gary said he hated
to read Shakespeare in class. Got some of his guys
to bang on their desks and throw their books around.

'It was so noisy, it was almost like a riot, Ma.
That's when Mr. Harrington...you know...'

'You weren't part of this Gary business, were you?'

'No, Ma, jeez, I wouldn't do that. I like Mr. Harrington,
I like Shakespeare class, too... the thing is...
well... no, never mind...it's okay...'

The boy puts his hands on the table as if he wants to leave,
but stays sitting. He wants to say what's bothering him.
She'll wait.

'It's just that I feel kind of bad,' the boy says,
'I didn't help him, Mr. Harrington. I don't know...
cause I was... I guess... afraid...'

Helpless, too, she thinks. She remembers how
she froze up with fear, couldn't stop Cousin Malkie
from smashing his hand through a window
when he lost his best friend to black lung.

'You did right' she tells the kid, 'not to butt in
when it won't help. When you're sure what you do
helps the other guy, that's when you stand up.'

That's what Harry would have told the kid.
Though naturally, he'd have backed it up
with a tickle and a song.

'Put your dishes in the sink now. And mind
you be careful. There's a streetlight out on Chandler.
Take your brains. Keep an eye out for trouble.'

Of course, there'll be trouble, she thinks.
It's all around them all the time.

1952

The Matchbook

This guy's a drinking man, she thinks.
Watery eyes, nose changing shape.

'Your young man is quite a talent,' he says,
leaning his beefy self forward on the kitchen table,
a put-on smile backing up his words.

A pencil sketch of a dark-haired full-lipped woman
lies on the tablecloth looking remarkably like the sketch
on the matchbook cover lying next to it.

'DRAW ME!' the matchbook reads, 'WIN $200!'

'This is fine work, son,' the man says,
affecting a fatherly pride. 'This is your lucky day,
the day we open the door to your future.'

'You must be proud,' he says to the mother,
his raspy voice hinting at tears.

The boy's eager. Looks to his mother with hope.

'That two hundred dollars isn't in cash, is it?'

The man is puzzled.

'The cover makes you think
the prize is cash. But the teeny-weeny print
on the bottom says it's for a scholarship.'

'That's right,' he says, almost a question.

'So, it's not really cash, is it?'

'Well, no, not exactly, but it's—'

'So, can you tell me, Howard,' she says,
calling him by name for the first time.
'How much are you going to soak us
for what you call a scholarship?'

Howard forces a wide nicotine grin, starts a routine
about what the program can do for the boy.

'I didn't ask what,' she says. 'I asked how much it costs.'

Taking this guy for a ride feels so good, she's unaware
of the what's-going-on-look that shows on the boy's face.

'Normally it's seven,' Howard says, still grinning.
'But the boy's won two, that's a nice chunk right there,
knocks it down to just five hundred.'

'We don't have five hundred dollars.'

'Well, that's all right,' he says, gets a contract
from his briefcase, holds it up like a gift. 'That's why
we have a payment plan for people who—'

'Plan or no plan, we don't have the money. Period.'

She speaks with such finality, Howard rises
with a grimace that wants to be a smile,
takes the unsigned contract and briefcase,
leaves as quickly as he can.

She's satisfied. Thinks what's done is best for the kid.

'Wasn't that some con job,' she says.

She gets no answer from the boy. He's staring at
the matchbook cover with a drawing of a dark-haired,
full-lipped woman that lies face up on the table.

Well, I blew that one, didn't I? she thinks.
I thought for sure he'd see what I was doing.
Goddamn it, we're in a mess again, aren't we?

The boy's still looking at the matchbook.

'I'll get supper ready,' she says.

The kid comes in to supper sulking,
sits scraping his fork on the plate.
Prince spaghetti and meatballs,
as cold as Mount Everest.

Still hurts over that matchbook con job, does he?

'You're a pain in the butt,' she says.
'Think how bad your father would feel
if he saw you moping like a sad sack.'

'Daddy's not here, you are,' he says.

'I did what I did for your sake. After old Howard
got what he wanted, they would have sent you
some crap in the mail that wasn't going to help you.
They were stringing us along to milk us for all they could.'

The boy is twirling his spaghetti, not looking at her.

'And if you're waiting to get a sorry from me,
you'll have to wait for the Second Coming.
Like it or don't, it's my job to look after you.'

'I can look after myself.'

'No you can't. You're fifteen, second year high school.
You're all questions, not enough answers.'

'I have answers,' he says. 'You just don't like them.'

'Is that right, smart guy? See if you can answer this one.
What are you going to do with your life?'

The boy takes his hands from his lap,
lays them flat on the table. His eyes are cold.

'Do you want to be a bag boy all your life?'

'I don't care,' he says, gets up to leave.

She's up from her chair. 'Where do you think you're
going!?'

'None of your business.'

'Don't smart-aleck me, buster. Sit down and shut up
or I'll whack you a good one.'

The boy looks right at her, then sits down, his bottom lip
pushed forward, the way he does when he pouts.

This is getting to be too much.
She doesn't like it, but she has to call Jonesy.

'Here's what's going to happen. You're going to use
your working papers for a good cause, your uncle Jonesy
will get you a part time job helping his mechanics.'

'No, I can't be a mechanic.'

'You need a trade to make a life.'

'I don't want a trade. I want to draw.'

'You want to be grounded again,' she says,
'I'd be happy to ground you again.'

'Jeez, Ma. All right, okay...'

'Just be sure you mind your manners in this house.'

'Okay. Can I be excused now?'

'If you put that bottom lip back where it belongs.'

'Okay, okay, okay!'

She reminds him curfew is nine.

She covers his cold spaghetti with a clean dish towel.
She'll reheat it when he gets home.

1953

The Foley Kid

Her spine stiffens the moment she sees
Tommy Foley and a few of his thugs from Southie
come into view of the window. Here they are,
acting like they own Berkeley Street,
skittering in and out of the street lights,
laughing, shouting, swearing, passing beer around.

Oh, my God. That's the kid with them!

Sirens scream, bells pound a fury in her head.

She grabs her black cloth coat, puts it over
her blue-checkered house dress,
rushes down the flight of steps in house slippers,
opens the door, runs to the corner,
slaps Tommy Foley across his face,
grabs the boy's arm, pushes him home
and to hell with what the neighbors say.

She shoves the boy on the sofa, tells him stay put,
don't say a word. Catches her breath to steady her mind
and ease the burn in her lungs.

'Give me your key.' Holds her hand out arm's length.
Raises her voice. 'The key, now!'

The boy doesn't move. 'You're deaf, are you?' she says.
'I said now. Now is now. The key.'

She pockets the key, hangs up her coat.

'You've got one more year of high school.
You don't graduate your life is done. Over and out.

Are you listening to what I say?'

The boy nods his answer.

'You can thank God and your lucky stars
I got you away from that son of a bitch
before he could get you in real trouble.'

The boy says he's sorry. She tells him
sorry's not good enough.

'I told you stay away from him, didn't I?
But here you are drinking behind my back.'

'No, Ma, I —'

'Don't lie. I saw you drinking Gansett.'

'It was just one sip one time, Ma.'

'Your mind is your own, isn't it? So grow up
and use it. How can you be so dumb
to get mixed up with him like that?'

He tells her it was an accident. He bumped into
Tommy outside a club on Huntington Ave.

'You can bet your sweet you-know-what,
there's more than meets the eye with Tommy Foley.
What were you doing up there?'

'Nothing, Ma...'

'Don't nothing me. Did you go in that club?'

'No, Ma, we're too young. They had jazz.
We just hung around outside, listening.'

'So, how come one minute you're up there,
the next minute you're down here drinking beer?'

'I don't know... it sort of just happened, I guess.'

'Don't play innocent. You know something.
You better tell me what it is.'

'I said I didn't know, didn't I?'

'And I'm not an idiot, am I? I know something went on, and
you know what it is. So, you don't tell me,
big as you are you'll get one hell of a whipping.'

'Well... all it was, was one of the players came out,
gave Tommy some money, Tommy gave him
a little bag of something, tobacco, I think... '

The sirens are wailing full blast, this is bad.
This is really bad.

'You're fifteen years old and you tell me,
with all your smarts, you don't know
the difference between tobacco and marijuana?'

Her mind's going crazy places.

Is the kid playing her for a fool?
Maybe he does it on purpose, like when
he quit the job Jonesy set up for him.
Or when he said he needed his weekends
to rehearse the spring play.
What if she's been wrong all this time
and the kid's been getting in trouble all along?

'You listen to me with both ears,' she says.

'If you're in on this, then you're an accessory,
guilty as them. Then up the river you go.'

'I didn't know, Ma, honest to God.
The only reason I stayed was the music
was so good I couldn't leave.'

'Why should I believe anything you say?'

'I swear, Ma. I'm telling the truth, I didn't know.'

'You want to swear on something,
you can swear on your father's grave.'

The boy's hands go up, palms out, to stop her.

'Swear it! Swear it on your father's grave!'

'I can't, Ma,' his eyes wet with tears,
'I just can't do that. Please...'

Images are crowding her mind. Ghostly griefs
wanting to be let in; Malkie smashing glass,
Harry's coffin, her coal-dusted da.

She narrows her eyes hard on the kid.
Speaks in a low, cold voice to stop the dam
from bursting out all the years of grief
she's kept secret from herself.

'The day that I find out you lied is the day
you're no son of mine. The day you pack
your things and find yourself another place to live.'

Neither one can move.

The boy is mute with pain.

The mother is drained. Blank.

'Well, never mind,' she says,
her voice absent any affect.
'Go to bed, get some rest.'

Sitting on the edge of her bed, she waits for sleep.

Maybe I was wrong, she thinks. Maybe it's me
who's the fool here. Maybe the kid isn't lying.
Maybe he's innocent, making a sap of himself
for the likes of Tommy Foley.

Fool or no fool, it's me who looks after the kid,
right or wrong, whether I believe him or not.

Well, there you go. I straightened out
that goddamn mess, didn't I now?

1954

At the Play

The scuffle of feet behind the red velvet curtain
jangles her nerves. What am I doing here?
I don't know the first thing about plays.

She'd planned to use Bingo as an excuse to not go,
but the kid was so excited for her to see him,
he'd already put a seat aside for her.

What do I do? What do I say afterwards? she thinks,
as the lights go down and the curtain opens.
Never mind, don't worry about that. This acting
is a good thing. Got the kid off the streets, didn't it?

The play doesn't make any sense. Some kids
dressed in fancy old-time clothes, trying to talk
like they're Brits. But then, she's no expert, is she?

Still, she can't take her eyes off her son.
It's strange. He's him. But he's not him.

After the play she stands by the exit door
waiting for the boy, watching family and friends
greet each other, shake hands, hug, kiss,
wait for their kids.

And here they come. Running into the lobby,
bouncing up and down, grabbing cake and soda,
chatter popping all around like popcorn machines;
more hubbub than Friday night at the Shamrock.

It's a different world from hers. More show-off
than she could ever be. Or wants to be, she thinks,
while she waits for the boy near the exit door.

The boy rushes out, wearing a grin like Harry's.
The girl who was his girlfriend in the play
is with him. The other actors crowd around them
clapping, whistling their congratulations.

She notices how the girl looks at him.

He sees his mother by the door, says something
to the girl. Makes his way toward her, the grin gone,
a question on his face.

'You okay, Ma?' he asks.

She manages to smile. 'Sure, why?'

'No, I just thought, I mean you were standing
by the door with your coat... so I thought...
you might be sick or something...?'

'Oh no,' she says, scrambling to ease things up,
'I thought I should wait a little bit. Let you enjoy
celebrating with your friends. And you know me,
I get antsy when I go too long without my smokes.
Thought I might sneak out for a puff or two.'

Shut up, she tells herself, you're talking too much.

'Yuh,' the boy says. Then, after a nervous pause,
'Well, I'm glad you came, Ma.'

'Promised I would, didn't I?'
That didn't come out how I wanted.
I'll botch this I don't get in a better mood.

'So...did you enjoy the play?' the boy asks.

'Oh yeah,' she answers. 'In case you didn't notice,
so did everybody else.'

'I guess I was pretty good then, huh?'

'Oh yeah. It was something you got all those bows, eh?'

'It was, yuh.' He looks over to the others gathered round
a table; leavings of cake and soda pop litter a blue and gold
paper tablecloth. The school colors, she guesses.

Two guys are singing, a girl in matching pink blouse
and knee-high skirt dances to 'Sh-Boom,' the others
clap and woo-woo them. The girl he came in with
stands on a chair, waving him to come back.

The song irritates her. It's on every damn station.
Nobody plays Buddy Clark anymore. And here's the kid
wanting to dance to it. What can you do? Times change.

'So. We're done fishing for compliments, are we?'

He locks his eyes to hers and says, 'Well,
you took the bait, didn't you, Ma?'

What's going on? She didn't mean to insult him.

He says a quick goodbye and rushes off to the girl.

She'd like to be happier for him than she is.

1955

Artie Shaughnessy

She never saw it coming. As far as she knew, everything was
hunky-dory. After graduation he and that girl were still going
steady, Jonesy was angling to get him a job
at City Hall. Benefits, pensions, the whole works.

And now he comes waltzing in and springs it on her without
so much as a how-do-you-do.

Says he's going to New York to be an actor.

Her feelings burst every which way, desperate
for this not to happen. It's a mess, a goddamn mess.

Two high school plays do not make him an actor.

No telling what will happen to him if he doesn't
wake up from this pipe dream. He'll be lost to a life
of lousy or no jobs, like every other Joe Schmoe
in this beaten down neighborhood. Nowhere to go
but down and done. Look at Artie Shaughnessy.
Thought he'd be a big football star, didn't he?
Had a full crowd for his send off at the Shamrock,
didn't make it out of training camp. Look at him now.
Poor bastard wanders around from bar to bar
like a ghost. Mooching drinks, talking glory days.
Pitiful. Man's left with no pride.

We're not Hollywood hot shots, we're workers.
What we do is work. The country would be up
shit's creek without a paddle if no one worked.

The boy is looking at her, waiting for her reaction.

It pops out of her mouth. 'Listen, big shot, just get a job,
a good girl, and get married.'

The boy stares at her, says nothing, then takes
the amber ashtray from the windowsill,
throws it to the floor at her feet.

Cigarette butts and ashes scatter on the parlor rug.
All hell breaks loose in her head.

She's so mad the force of the slap she meant
for the side of his face bloodies his nose.

'For Christ's sake, look what you made me do.'

'I knew you would,' he says, his voice ice cold.

She feels his eyes boring into hers, rattling her mind,
reading her thoughts, searching her secrets.

'Knew I would what?' she says, the question a demand.

'I knew you would try to stop me.'

'What the hell are you talking about?'

'I knew it when you came to the play.'

This isn't hurt or anger for her anymore.
It's plain old fear. She knew it, too, didn't she?
He was already gone then, wasn't he?

'Go clean yourself up,' she says.
'You're getting blood on the rug.'

She releases the smoke from her lungs
as St Vincent's closes up shop
and a few rooms light up at the Earle.

Well, she thinks, that was one hell of a blowout.

She takes a sip of Four Roses, thinking
it's the first time she's had a drink at home
since the boy came back from the Peabody.

She takes a deep drag on her cigarette, pays no mind
to the cough she hacks as she exhales, stabs it out
in the retrieved and clean amber ashtray.

Only three cigs left, she thinks. First time I won't
send the kid to the corner for a new pack.

Thank god, she's got work tomorrow.
Maybe she'll ask around. Pick up more jobs.
Tomorrow night, she'll meet Peggy and Joyce
for Bingo at St. Michael's.

To hell with it. What's done is done.

Twilight fades to dusk on Berkeley Street.
The street lights come on.

1975

Thanksgiving

She's in a good mood. Good day today.
Kid's plane is in from New York.
The first time he'll visit her
at the apartment in Old Colony.

It's a mess getting from Logan to here.
She worries he'll get stuck in traffic.
Checks the wall clock she brought
from Berkeley Street, whiles away
the waiting time making sure
the place is spotless for his arrival.

She'd been worried about subsidized housing,
but Sally and Jonesy had been right.
It's not too bad for city housing.

Smaller, yeah, but no stairs to climb.
And people here are nicer. Not like the old days
when nobody gave a rat's bum if you were poor.

She can still get around a bit, cook a little.
Keep a clean house. Get out on days
it's not too cold for the emphysema.

Sally and Jonesy will sometimes come by
with enough Chinese food for leftovers,
or drive her to Castle Island for fried clams.

And there's Delilah, comes in from City Services
twice a week to check on her, see she's okay,
take her blood pressure and the like.

Outside of that, not too many highlights,

no Bingo with Peggy and Joyce these days,
no Berkeley Street shenanigans,
no kid to keep out of trouble.

Not much fun digging up the past, is it?
But what's an old girl to do, eh?

She checks the clock again, figures
it's close to time. Sits by the window
to watch for the cab that brings him
to Old Colony.

Isn't he the spitting image of Harry himself
coming through the door and kissing her hand
like she's the queen of England. She wasn't
so glad to see him, she'd tell him to cut the crap.

'Got through the traffic all right, did you?'

'I did. Sumner Tunnel wasn't too bad today.'

'Lucky you. Did I remember to tell you
there's only one bedroom, you've got the couch?'

'Oh, sorry, Ma,' he says, 'I thought I told you I had to catch a
plane back tonight for rehearsal tomorrow.'

'Oh, well, you probably did, The old noggin's
not too good with memory these days.
Anyway, you must be tired. Maybe you want
to take a minute and freshen up before dinner.'

'I would, Ma. Thanks.'

'I'll make us some coffee.'

'That would be great, Ma.'

When he's gone with his travel kit,
she takes a peek at the hand he kissed.

She hasn't seen him much since he left for New York.
He'd make it back once, twice a year, have coffee,
a little small talk. Other times he'd send a card,
the occasional phone call. She never asked him,
but he always left something for the rent.
Not that she needs it for how little the city charges.

Maybe it was her birthday last time she saw him.
Said he just got a Broadway show. Something
about a bunch of drunks in a bar. He wanted her
to fly up for the opening, but she wasn't feeling...
no... no, last time had to be when he came up
from his movie in Utah or someplace, for...
Christ. It was my operation, wasn't it?

How in the name of Saint Teresa could a person
forget a thing like that? Well, nobody would want
to remember they took out some of your intestines.

After he's cleaned up, her son sips instant coffee
in a kitchenette that barely sits the two of them.

'Thanksgiving dinner's on Jonesy,' she says.
'It's at Farragut House.'

'Are you okay with going out, Ma?
You're not getting around so well.'

'Don't worry yourself, I'm not done yet.'

'Still the tough old bird, are you?'

'I'll take the tough, leave out the old bird,'

she says and gets up to rinse his cup.

She doesn't say she's ashamed for not being able
to cook Thanksgiving dinner for him.
Last time she was up to it was last year,
back on Berkeley Street, for Peggy and Joyce.

After dinner, tired and wheezy
from a little bit of turkey and a few sips
of amber ale, she eases down into her chair.

'You're looking worn out, Ma,' her son says.
'Want me to get your oxygen?'

'I hate that goddamn thing, reminds me
of the hospital. Move it next to the bed for me,
I'll stick it in my nose later.'

She closes her eyes. Dozes off
to a kaleidoscope of images
swirling round and round: her da
coughing blood, the boy
sleeping in his crib, a couple
smooching in funny hats, Harry
singing I'll get by, a paper boat
of clams, a ferry captain
in a supper club, Sally
sneaking a nip, men in groups,
a hospital sign, Malkie's dark eyes,
a band leader in white tuxedo,
a crucifix floating in fog, her ma
brushing somebody's hair,
hers or maybe Cousin Margaret's...
coming, going, coming again.

'You asleep, Ma?' her son whispers.

In a half-awake haze, she imagines him
past and present at the same time;
a grown man in a chair and a wide-eyed boy
standing on the prow of a ferry, thinking
this is me here, that is them there.

Oh, sweet Mother of Jesus! Ain't that a wonder
to behold! Not a kid now, is he though? she thinks,
fully awake to the grown man across from her.

'You were dozing,' he says. 'Too much fun, huh?'

'Better than no fun at all, eh?'

She wants to do something, doesn't know what.
She just wants to do it. 'Get that bottle of Four Roses
from under the kitchen cabinet.'

'You sure about the hard stuff, Ma? You hardly
sipped your ale at Farragut House.'

'Just a little nip. For Thanksgiving.
Bring us two shots. Not too big on mine.'

She takes the whiskey he brings her and says,
'You look like your father you know.'

'Really? Do I?'

'You do. Right down to that bald spot
on the back of your head.' He grins,
pats the bald spot. 'I'll drink to that.'

Even a little sip like this goes down too hard
these days, she thinks. Notices he looks
at his watch; thinks how, in the beginning, the slow coming
and the fast leaving used to bother her,

but she's okay with it now. He's an actor,
for God's sake. A job that keeps you on the move.

He puts his glass down, glances toward
the window that looks out to the walkway.

'Relax,' she says, 'the cabbie will beep
when he gets here. Finish up your whiskey,
it'll make the trip easier.'

'You're right,' he says taking the last sip.
'You know, I'm really sorry to go, Ma,
but I can't miss tomorrow's rehearsal.'

'No need to be sorry,' she says. 'You have a right
to earn a living like anybody else, don't you?'

'Listen, Ma,' he says, 'before I go, I just want...'
The kid looks a little nervous, makes her nervous.
'The thing is, Ma,' he continues, 'well... I just
wanted to say that I—'

'Never mind that,' she says, taking as deep a breath
as her lungs will allow. 'You don't need to say anything, I
don't either. What's mine is mine, yours is yours.'

'I know, Ma, but I would—'

'All things considered, we're doing okay, aren't we?
Let's keep it that way. Short and sweet.'

'Jeez, Ma,' he says with a chuckle. 'You've sure
got a way with words. That was pretty damn blunt.'

'Just trying to get the job done the right way.'

'Yup. Have to play it the way they wrote it, don't we?'

'Better that way,' she says.

'Okay with me, if it's okay with you.'

'So, we're good then, are we?'

'Yeah, Ma. We're good.'

'Okay then,' she says, 'It's you off to work,
and this old girl off to bed.'

She turns down his offer for help. She'll do it herself,
tells him to get himself another nip of Four Roses
for the road. Reminds him to put the glasses in the sink and
the bottle back under it.

Her room is spare: a crucifix,
some framed photos on the wall,
water and rosary on the bedside table.

Leaves the oxygen tank off.
Doesn't want to hear the hissing.

God, she's tired. Even the little she ate
at Farragut House was too much for her.
The old stomach works too hard these days.

Her fingers work their way, bead to bead,
through the rosary as she whispers a novena
for Holy Mother Mary to look after her son.

Minutes later, she hears him come to the door,
hesitate, then open it a crack, but not come in.

An ether of sorrow permeates the air,
gently bathes away the clouds of fog;

she remembers sitting at the Berkeley Street
window, smoking, lost in yearning for Harry,
as the radio played 'I'll get by, as long as I have you...'

My God... the kid was there then too, wasn't he?
Didn't say a word then either. Just stood there and
watched me. Hmm... what about that...

Drowsing off, she worries the kid
will miss his plane... no... it's not a plane...
he's on a ferry, isn't he...

a peculiar thought, or maybe just a feeling,
comes to her—
that her and the boy are more than blood,
more like orphans than mother and son.

On their own, but for the luck of finding each other.

The November day deepens into early evening dark;
a security light from the service area glows behind
her back window.

All that remains is the shadow of its frame
fallen across her room, and the faint sound
of a motor fading away in the distance.

Acknowledgments

My grateful thanks to Paul Bowers of Turning Plow Press, whose keen eye and elegant mind have guided this manuscript to publication. And to the many friends and writers who, over the years, have read parts of *Mother and Son*. I am especially indebted to the Oklahoma writing community for their support and encouragement. A particular thank you to those who host public readings in bookstores, bars and diners, private homes, art galleries and train stations, colleges and universities throughout the region, whose hard work creates audiences, fosters love for the spoken word, and quite often shows a writer where rewrites are needed.

And a special thanks to my wife, Rilla Askew, and my niece, Cherie Austin McGaughey, whose love of family is a continuing source of inspiration for me.

About the Author

Paul Austin's book *Spontaneous Behavior, the Art and Craft of Acting* was published by Turning Plow Press in October 2022. His collection of prose and poetry *Notes on Hard Times* was published by Village Books Press. His work has appeared in such publications as *This Land*, *Sugar Mule*, *Oklahoma Review*, *More Monologues by Men*, and *Newport Review*. His poems have also been included in *Speak Your Mind*, the 2019 anthology of Woody Guthrie Poets, *Bull Buffalo and Indian Paintbrush*, an anthology of Oklahoma poetry, *Behind the Mask: Haiku in the Time of Covid-19*, *Jerry Jazz Musician*, and *Level Land: Poems for and about the I-35 Corridor*. *Late Night Conspiracies*, a collection of his writings, was performed with jazz ensemble at New York's Ensemble Studio Theatre.

Mother and Son

by Paul Austin